WORLD CUP CLOSE-UP

MEN'S SOCCER ON THE BIGGEST STAGE

by Kurt Waldendorf

CAPSTONE PRESS
a capstone imprint

Published by Capstone Press, an imprint of Capstone
1710 Roe Crest Drive, North Mankato, Minnesota 56003
capstonepub.com

Library of Congress Cataloging-in-Publication Data is available on the Library of Congress website

ISBN: 979-8-8752-6989-9 (hardcover)
ISBN: 979-8-8752-6984-4 (paperback)
ISBN: 979-8-8752-6985-1 (ebook PDF)

Summary: The World Cup is an international meeting of the greatest soccer players on the planet. Soccer fans can explore a crash course on this pinnacle event, from its historic beginnings to its modern-day, technology-filled future.

Editorial Credits
Editor: Heather DiLorenzo Williams; Designer: Cynthia Della-Rovere; Media Researchers: Courtney Rust, Catherine Guden

Image Credits
Getty Images: Alex Grimm, cover (left), Anthony Bibard/FEP/Icon Sport, cover (right), Ayman Aref/NurPhoto, 18, Catherine Ivill, 20, Clive Brunskill, 12, Harold Cunningham/FIFA, 29, Joris Verwijst/BSR Agency, cover (middle), Kenta Harada, 19, Keystone/Hulton Archive, 7, Laurence Griffiths, 5, Marcelo Endelli, cover (top), Matias Baglietto/NurPhoto, 17, Mike Hewitt/FIFA, 13, Mohammed Dabbous/Anadolu, 14-15, Noushad Thekkayil/NurPhoto, 27, PytyCzech/iStock, 16, Richard Sellers/Sportsphoto/Allstar, 23, Santiago Mazzarovich/picture alliance, 8, Simon Bruty/Anychance, 24; Newscom:The Netherlands V Gibraltar/ZUMAPRESS, 21; Shutterstock: Carlo Kaminski, 10–11

Design Elements
Shutterstock: Shutterstock: Arroyan Art, Dmitry Rukhlenko, Donglpix, madorf, Vector-3D

Printed and bound in China. 6459

CONTENTS

Chapter 1
THE BIGGEST STAGE FOR THE BIGGEST GAME — 4

Chapter 2
WORLD CUP HISTORY — 6

Chapter 3
THE WORLD CUP TODAY — 12

Chapter 4
CROWNING A CHAMPION — 20

Chapter 5
A GOLDEN FUTURE — 26

GLOSSARY 30
READ MORE 31
INTERNET SITES 31
INDEX 32
ABOUT THE AUTHOR 32

CHAPTER 1

THE BIGGEST STAGE FOR THE BIGGEST GAME

The World Cup is one of the biggest sporting events on Earth. Every four years, millions of people travel to cheer on their favorite men's **national teams** at the tournament. Host countries often build new stadiums just for the event. In 2022, about 5 billion people around the world tuned in to watch matches on TV or online.

The tournament is successful for many reasons. One is the popularity of the sport. Around 240 million people play soccer, and about 3.5 billion people consider themselves soccer fans, the most of any game. Another is the World Cup's reputation. Many countries have soccer championships. But only winners of the World Cup can say they are men's soccer world champions.

Australia and Argentina battle for the ball during the Round of 16 at the 2022 World Cup. Millions of fans from around the world traveled to Qatar to watch their teams compete.

CHAPTER 2

WORLD CUP HISTORY

The World Cup hasn't always been so big. The event is the result of more than 100 years of **international** competition.

Early Events

The idea for a world championship goes back to the early days of soccer. The sport first became popular in England and Scotland. The first international match was in 1872. The countries faced off to see who had the top team. Soon, soccer spread to more countries. A bigger competition was needed. A group called the Fédération Internationale de Football Association (FIFA) was formed. FIFA oversees international soccer competitions.

Uruguay's team, pictured here, won the first-ever World Cup in 1930.

In 1914, the Olympic Games became the men's soccer world championship. But FIFA was not happy with the event. Olympic rules kept some players from competing. So FIFA president Jules Rimet started a new event. The first World Cup was set for 1930.

Estadio Centenario was opened in 1930 for the first World Cup. In honor of the stadium's history, World Cup organizers announced that it would host the opening match of the 2030 tournament.

The First World Cup

For the World Cup to last, it needed to get off on the right foot. FIFA picked the country of Uruguay to host. Soccer was popular in South America. Uruguay had also agreed to build a stadium for the event.

But the tournament faced challenges. Travel from Europe took more than two weeks. The boat carrying Egypt's team got caught in a storm. The team had to turn back. In the end, only 13 teams made the trip. Still, the event was a success. More than 90,000 fans watched Uruguay take on Argentina in the final.

FAST FACT

Uruguay's new stadium was called Estadio Centenario. The name referred to 100 years of the country's **independence**. Nearly 100 years later, the building is still home to Uruguay's national team.

An Expanding Tournament

Soccer kept growing in the second half of the century. In 1954, about 40 countries had men's national teams. By 1998, the number had grown to 174. The World Cup grew too. A whopping 32 teams competed in the 1998 event.

FIFA brought the World Cup to more places. Mexico hosted North America's first tournament in 1970. In 2002, Japan and South Korea hosted Asia's first World Cup. And in 2010, South Africa became Africa's first host country.

Finding the Right Format

FIFA also tried different formats for the event. In 1958, they found one that stuck. The 16 teams were broken into groups of four. During the **group stage**, each team played the other three squads in the group. The top two moved on to the next round. Fans loved the format. Each team was sure to play at least three games.

South African soccer fans gear up to watch the first game of the 2010 World Cup. The tournament was played in 10 different stadiums across South Africa.

CHAPTER 3

THE WORLD CUP TODAY

The World Cup is now more competitive than ever. To be successful, countries, teams, and players spend years preparing.

Choosing a Host

Hosting the World Cup is a big honor. The host country gets to show off its cities and culture. The event brings many visitors who help the country's economy. Hosting also gives the country's team an automatic spot in the tournament.

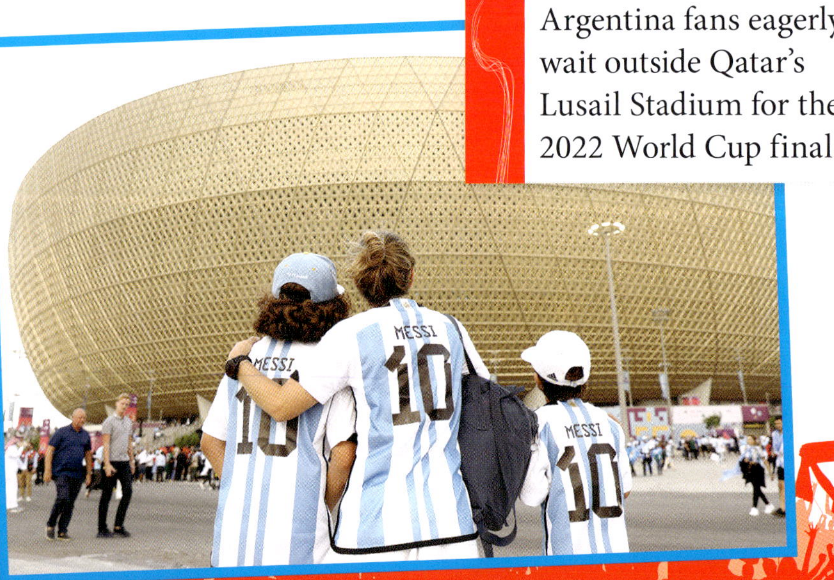

Argentina fans eagerly wait outside Qatar's Lusail Stadium for the 2022 World Cup final.

FIFA officials announce Canada, Mexico, and the United States as the hosts of the 2026 World Cup.

A host is chosen up to 10 years before the event. Countries send in **bids** laying out their plans. In 2018, Canada, Mexico, and the United States sent in a bid together. All three countries were picked to host the 2026 tournament. It was the first time three nations were chosen to host.

Setting the Stage

Once the host is set, the work begins. Countries may need to improve stadiums. Or they may need to build new ones altogether. Hosts also build places for visitors to stay. They create ways for people to get to the stadiums. The 2022 World Cup was the costliest ever. Qatar spent $220 billion on the event.

Spreading out the event can lower the cost. Sixteen different cities were chosen to host the 2026 World Cup. No new stadiums were planned.

Stadium 974

Qatar built seven new stadiums for the 2022 World Cup. Among them, Stadium 974 was unique. It was designed to be taken down after the event. The stadium was built using 974 shipping containers. This allows it to be deconstructed and shipped to future events.

Stadium 974 hosted seven matches during the 2022 World Cup in Qatar.

FIFA CONFEDERATIONS

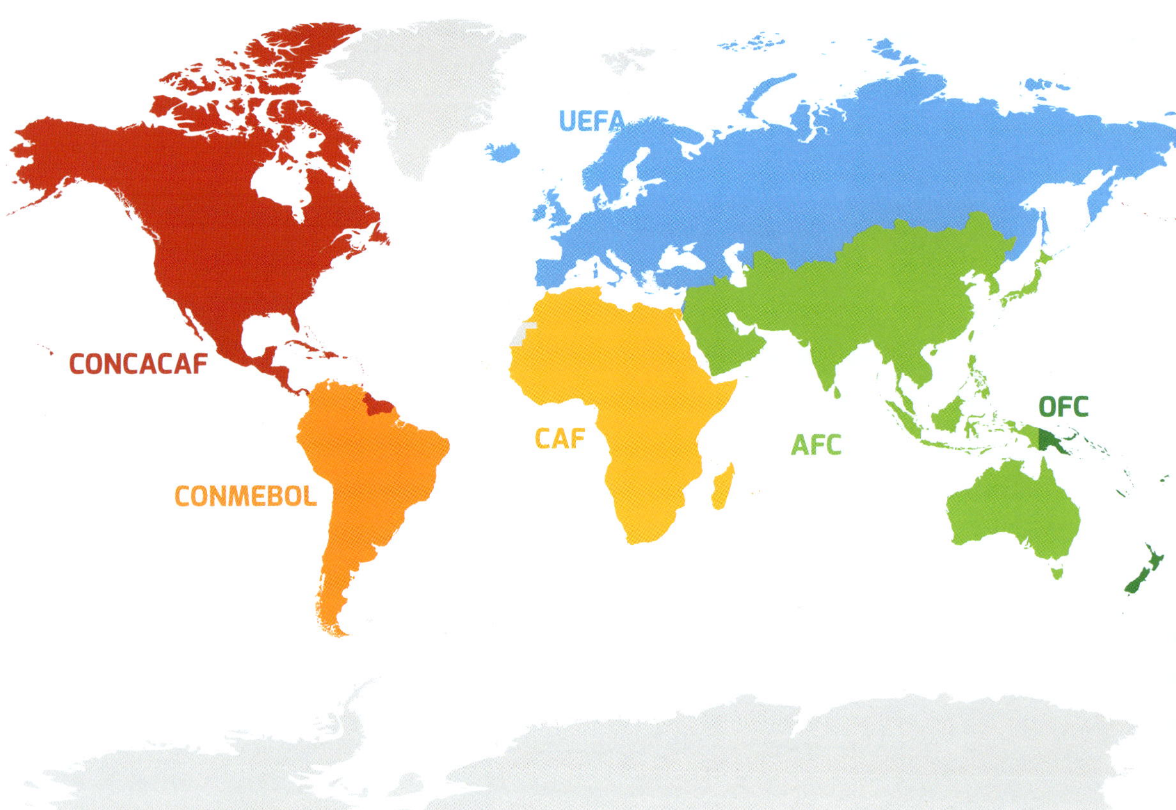

Making the Cut

For teams, getting ready for the World Cup starts with **qualifying**. FIFA divides all national teams into regions. Teams from each region play against one another in the years leading up to the World Cup. The top teams from each region earn spots in the tournament.

For the 2026 World Cup, FIFA expanded the tournament to 48 teams. But competition was stiff, with more than 200 nations trying to secure a spot.

After a team has qualified, they play in matches called friendlies. These games do not count for the tournament. But they aren't just for fun, either. Managers use the matches to try out different lineups, strategies, and players.

Argentina soccer legend Lionel Messi (right) competes against Peru in a World Cup qualifying match in 2024.

Brazil celebrates their win over Korea Republic in the Round of 16 at the 2022 World Cup. Brazil is the only nation that has qualified for every World Cup since the tournament began.

Japan celebrates a win over Bahrain in 2025. The win qualified Japan to compete in the 2026 World Cup.

Player Preparations

Some players take part in multiple World Cups. But many only get the opportunity one time. Players spend years training to compete at the highest level. They work on speed, strength, and endurance. They also train their brains, learning to handle the pressure of top competition.

Making it onto a national team is just the first step. During qualifying, each player competes for a place on the final **roster**. Final rosters are set a week before the World Cup. Only the top 23 players from each nation make the trip.

Teams arrive in the host nation early. They adjust to the time zone, weather, and **altitude**. Then they get ready to go against the best of the best.

CHAPTER 4

CROWNING A CHAMPION

When the tournament kicks off, players put their training to work. National teams face off in matches. After more than 100 matches are played, a world champion is crowned.

Fair Play

The players aren't the only ones who need to be at the top of their game at the World Cup. Game officials must be physically fit and knowledgeable about soccer rules. Every penalty, offside, and out-of-bounds call can make a big difference. Only the top referees are picked for the event.

The stadium displays let fans know what plays are being reviewed.

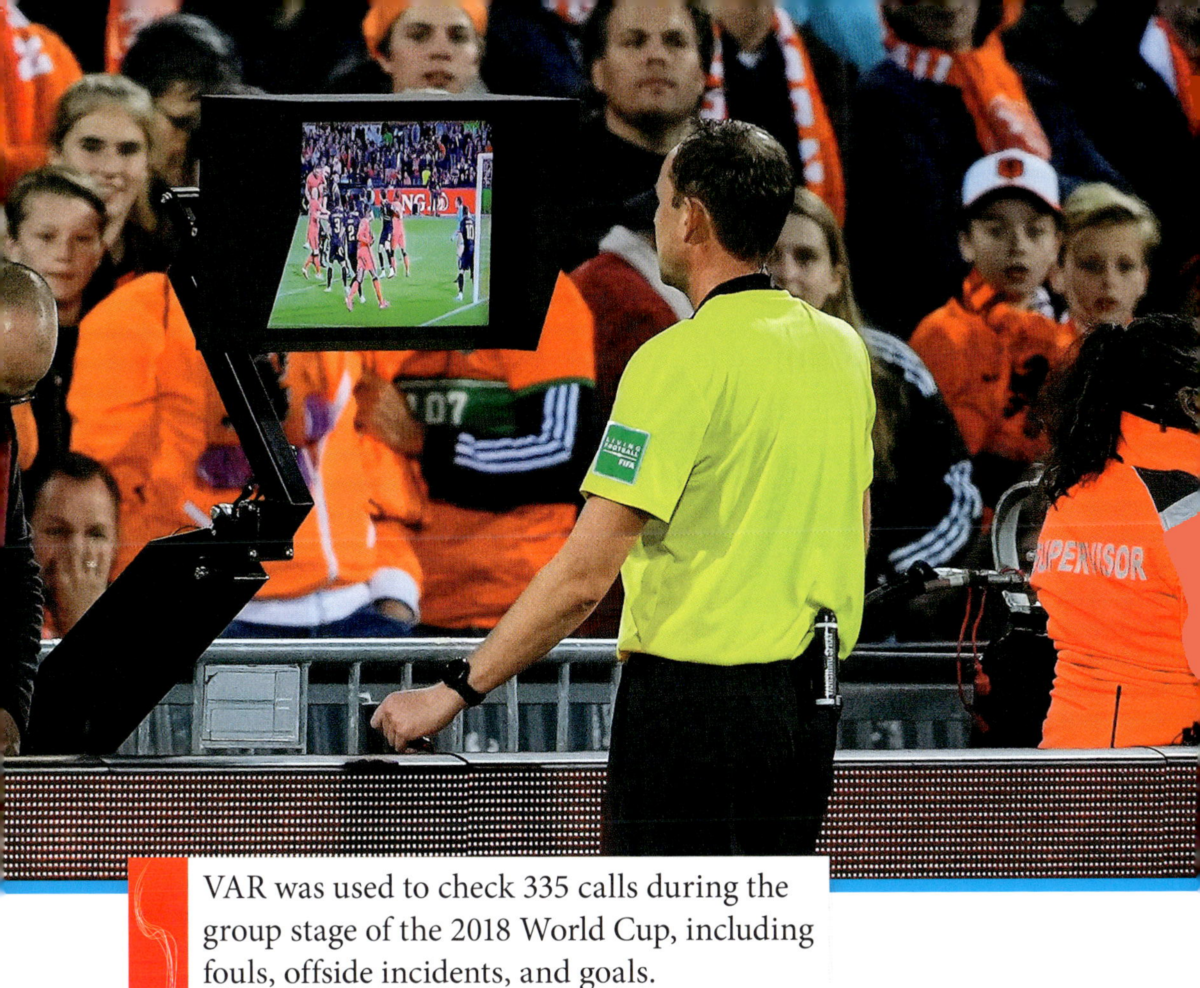

VAR was used to check 335 calls during the group stage of the 2018 World Cup, including fouls, offside incidents, and goals.

Technology also plays a role. In 2018, a Video Assistant Referee (VAR) was introduced. This off-the-field referee uses cameras to review key plays. Then in 2022, a high-tech soccer ball was added. A sensor tracks the ball's exact location. Referees on the field use data from the ball and video replay to make the right calls in the most important moments.

A Select Group

Teams that make it past the group stage enter the knockout stages. Any loss in these rounds ends a team's chance at a title. After these rounds, the last two teams standing face off in the final.

The final takes place on the last day of the event. The winning nation takes home the FIFA World Cup trophy and prize money. Players from the first, second, and third-place teams also receive a medal.

Tracking Progress

To perform their best, players need to take care of their bodies. The FIFA Player App was introduced at the 2022 tournament. The app measures how fast and far players move on the field. One player ran more than 10 miles (16 kilometers) in a match in 2022. Information from the app helps players stay at their best throughout the event.

Heading into the 2026 World Cup, only eight countries had won the trophy. Brazil had the most titles with five. Germany and Italy each had four. Argentina had three. France and Uruguay each had two. And England and Spain each had one.

Although other countries have risen to the top of FIFA's rankings, Brazil is considered one of the most successful soccer teams of all time.

Lionel Messi, Emi Martínez, and Kylian Mbappé accept their individual awards at the 2022 World Cup.

Individual Awards

Playing in the World Cup is a team effort. Every player's goal is to lift the trophy for their country. Still, FIFA honors players who have top individual performances.

The Golden Ball is given to the event's best player. Argentina's Lionel Messi is the only person to take home the award more than once. He won it in 2014 and 2022. The Golden Boot goes to the top scorer. The Golden Glove is given to the best goalkeeper. France's Kylian Mbappé won the Golden Boot in 2022. Argentina's Emi Martínez won the 2022 Golden Glove.

Not many players win the World Cup. Even fewer go on to win as a manager. Only three men have won in both roles: Mário Zagallo of Brazil, Franz Beckenbauer of Germany, and Didier Deschamps of France.

CHAPTER 5

A GOLDEN FUTURE

The World Cup has changed a lot since the first event in 1930. The event will keep changing in the future.

Bigger and Better

Men's soccer continues to grow. Large countries such as the United States, India, and China have been slow to take up the game. But the number of people playing and watching soccer in each country is going up. Organizers of the 2026 World Cup scheduled matches in 11 U.S. cities. Planners hoped the big event would bring even more attention to soccer in the country. The sport also continues to grow in nations such as Japan, Indonesia, and Chile. As a result, fans might spot different teams competing in future World Cup finals.

Qatar's Lucas Mendes (right) battles Joel Kojo of Kyrgyzstan for the ball during a World Cup qualifying match. Qualifying for the 2026 World Cup started in 2023.

A 100-Year Celebration

Like they did with the 2026 World Cup, FIFA picked more than one country to host the 2030 event. Spain, Portugal, and Morocco were chosen to host.

FIFA also added something special to mark the World Cup's 100th year. They planned matches in Argentina, Paraguay, and Uruguay. A special match was planned for Estadio Centenario, the same stadium where the 1930 final was played. In all, 23 stadiums across six countries were chosen to host games. The plan was a fitting celebration for a global game.

In 2024, FIFA announced that Saudi Arabia would host the World Cup in 2034. It would be the Middle East's second time hosting in only 12 years. Because so many countries were committed to roles in the 2030 games, Saudi Arabia was the only nation to make a bid.

FIFA president Gianni Infantino announces the hosts of the 2030 World Cup at a FIFA event in 2024.

GLOSSARY

altitude (AL-ti-tood)—how high a place is above sea level

bids (BIDZ)—for the World Cup, countries' offers to host the tournament

group stage (GROOP STAYJ)—part of a tournament in which teams play multiple matches against a small set of competitors

independence (in-di-PEN-duhnss)—freedom from another country's rule

international (in-tur-NASH-uh-nuhl)—including more than one nation

national teams (NASH-uh-nuhl TEEMZ)—sports squads that represent their countries

qualifying (KWAHL-uh-fye-ing)—a series of games to determine which teams will play in the World Cup, or the act of winning enough matches to earn a place in the tournament

roster (ROSS-tur)—a list of players on a team

READ MORE

Flynn, Brendan. *The World Soccer Encyclopedia.* Minneapolis. ABDO, 2024.

Kerry, Isaac. *What You Never Knew About Lionel Messi.* North Mankato, MN. Capstone, 2023.

Marthaler, Jon. *The Best Teams of World Soccer.* Minneapolis. ABDO, 2024.

INTERNET SITES

ESPN: FIFA World Cup
www.espn.com/soccer/league/_/name/fifa.world

FIFA World Cup 2026
www.fifa.com/en/tournaments/mens/worldcup
/canadamexicousa2026

Sports Illustrated Kids: Soccer
www.sikids.com/tag/soccer

INDEX

Argentina, 9, 23, 25, 28

Beckenbauer, Franz, 25
Brazil, 23, 25

Canada, 13

England, 6, 23
Estadio Centenario, 9, 28

FIFA (Fédération Internationale de Football Association), 6–7, 9–10, 16–17, 22, 25, 28
France, 23, 25

Germany, 23, 25

Italy, 23

Mbappé, Kylian, 25
Messi, Lionel, 25
Mexico, 10, 13
Morocco, 28

Olympic Games, 7

Portugal, 28

Qatar, 14–15

Rimet, Jules, 7

Saudi Arabia, 28
Scotland, 6
Spain, 23, 28
Stadium 974, 15

United States, 13, 26
Uruguay, 9, 23, 28

Video Assistant Referee (VAR), 21

Zagallo, Mário, 25

About the Author

Kurt Waldendorf is the author of more than a dozen books for children. When he's not writing or editing, he enjoys indoor rock climbing and running along the shore of Lake Michigan with his dog. He lives in Chicago.